Mrs BEETON'S
HOME COOKING

POULTRY
DISHES

60p

WARD LOCK LIMITED · LONDON

© Ward Lock Limited 1986

First published in Great Britain
in 1986 by Ward Lock Limited,
8 Clifford Street,
London W1X 1RB,
an Egmont Company.

Edited by Susan Dixon
Designed by Melissa Orrom
Text filmset in Caslon 540
by Cheney & Sons Limited
Printed and bound in Italy by
L.E.G.O.

**British Library Cataloguing in
Publication Data**

Poultry.—
(Mrs. Beeton's home cooking)
  1. Cookery (Poultry)
  I. Series
  641.6'65   TX750

  ISBN 0-7063-6456-2

Notes
The recipes in this book have
been tested in metric weights
and measures. These have
been based on equivalents of
25g to 1 oz, 500g to 1 lb and
500ml to 1 pint, with some
adjustments where necessary.

  It is important to follow *either*
the metric *or* the imperial
measures. Do not use a
combination of measures.

POULTRY

A noble dish is a turkey, roast or boiled.
A Christmas dinner, with the middle
classes of this empire, would scarcely be
a Christmas dinner without its turkey;
and we can hardly imagine an object of
greater envy than is presented by a
respected portly paterfamilias carving, at
the season devoted to good cheer and
genial charity, his own fat turkey, and
carving it well.

Isabella Beeton 1861

On pages 2 and 3
From the back, clockwise
Chicken Kiev (page 12), *Braised Turkey (page 48)* and
Duckling in Red Wine (page 53)

CHICKEN

ROAST CHICKEN WITH HONEY AND ALMONDS

———— *4–6 helpings* ————

1 roasting chicken
½ lemon
salt and pepper
3 × 15ml spoons/3 tablespoons
  honey

50g/2oz blanched almonds
a pinch of powdered saffron
  (optional)
2 × 15ml spoons/2 tablespoons oil

Truss the chicken. Rub all over with the cut lemon, then sprinkle with salt and pepper. Line a roasting tin with a piece of foil large enough to cover the bird and to meet over the top. Put the bird on the foil, and rub it all over with honey. Slice the almonds and sprinkle them and the saffron, if used, over the bird. Pour the oil over the bird very gently. Wrap it completely in the foil, keeping it clear of the skin. Seal by folding over the edges. Roast in a moderate–fairly hot oven, 180–190°C/350–375°F/Gas 4–5, for about 1½ hours, until tender. Unwrap the foil for the last 10 minutes to allow the breast to brown.

Roast Chicken with Honey and Almonds

HOT CHICKEN LIVER MOUSSE

4 helpings

1 × 15ml spoon/1 tablespoon
   butter *or* margarine
2 × 15ml spoons/2 tablespoons
   plain flour
150ml/¼ pint milk
salt and pepper
225g/8oz chicken livers

1 egg
1 egg yolk
3 × 15ml spoons/3 tablespoons
   double cream
1 × 15ml spoon/1 tablespoon dry
   sherry
butter for greasing

GARNISH

chopped chives

Put the butter or margarine in a medium-sized saucepan with the flour and milk. Whisking all the time over a moderate heat, bring to the boil and cook for 2–3 minutes until thickened and smooth. Season to taste. Leave the sauce to become cold, stirring from time to time.

Remove the skin and tubes from the livers. Either process in an electric blender, or mince twice to obtain a purée. Beat in the egg and egg yolk. Add the sauce, cream and sherry. Pour into 4 well-buttered 150ml/¼ pint cocotte dishes. Place in a baking tin, and fill it with enough boiling water to come half-way up the sides of the dishes. Cook in a moderate oven, 180°C/350°C/Gas 4, for 25–30 minutes until a fine skewer inserted in the centre comes out clean. Allow to stand for a few minutes before turning out. Sprinkle with chives and serve hot.

BUTTER-DISH.

STUFFED CHICKEN LEGS

4 helpings

4 cooked drumsticks
salt and Cayenne pepper
1 × 15ml spoon/1 tablespoon
   vegetable oil
2 × 15ml spoons/2 tablespoons
   white breadcrumbs
1 × 2.5ml spoon/½ teaspoon
   mixed herbs

1 × 5ml spoon/1 teaspoon chopped
   parsley
1 small onion
1 × 2.5ml spoon/½ teaspoon
   grated lemon rind
1 egg
4 gammon rashers
fat for greasing

GARNISH

parsley sprigs

Season each drumstick with salt and Cayenne pepper and moisten with oil. Mix the breadcrumbs, herbs, and finely chopped parsley in a basin. Skin, blanch, and chop the onion finely and add it to the basin together with the lemon rind. Moisten the mixture with the egg. Spread each gammon rasher with this stuffing, and wrap one rasher around each drumstick. Tie or skewer the rasher securely in place. Put the drumsticks on a greased baking tray and cook in a moderate oven, 180°C/350°F/Gas 4, for 20 minutes; then cover them with foil, and cook for a further 20 minutes. Garnish with parsley sprigs.

Serve at once on trimmed slices of hot buttered toast.

QUICK CURRIED CHICKEN OR FOWL

(Country Captain)

1 cooked chicken *or* fowl
2 large onions
50g/2oz chicken fat *or* butter
1 × 15ml spoon/ 1 tablespoon curry powder
1 × 10ml spoon/1 dessertspoon curry paste
1 × 15ml spoon/1 tablespoon flour
375ml/¾ pint stock

1 large sweet apple
1 × 10ml spoon/1 dessertspoon chutney
1 × 15ml spoon/1 tablespoon lemon juice
salt and pepper
50g/2oz whole blanched almonds
fat for frying

GARNISH

lemon butterflies

Cut the bird into neat pieces. Keep any bones and trimmings for stock. Skin and chop the onions. Heat the chicken fat or butter, and fry the onions slowly until lightly browned. Add the curry powder, paste, and flour, and fry gently for 3 minutes. Stir in the stock gradually and bring to the boil. Peel, core, and dice the apple, and add to the mixture, together with the chutney, lemon juice, and seasoning. Simmer gently for 30 minutes, stirring occasionally. Add the chicken pieces and heat through slowly. Re-season if required.

Fry the almonds for a few minutes until golden-brown. Serve the chicken curry on a hot dish with the almonds sprinkled on top. Garnish with lemon butterflies.

Plain boiled rice and chutney should be served separately as accompaniments.

Quick Curried Chicken

CHICKEN KIEV

4 helpings

4 chicken breast and wing joints
salt and pepper
flour for coating

1 egg
100g/4oz soft white breadcrumbs
  (approx)
fat *or* oil for deep frying

BUTTER FILLING

finely grated rind of ½ lemon
1 × 15ml spoon/1 tablespoon
  chopped parsley
100g/4oz softened butter

salt and freshly ground black
  pepper
2 small cloves garlic

GARNISH

lemon wedges

parsley sprigs

Make the butter filling first. Work the lemon rind and parsley thoroughly into the butter, and season to taste. Crush and work in the garlic. Form the butter into a roll, wrap in clingfilm and chill.

To prepare the chicken, cut off the wing pinions. Turn the joints, flesh side up, and cut out all bones except the wing bone which is left in place. Do not cut right through the flesh. Flatten out the boned meat, cover with greaseproof paper, and beat lightly with a cutlet bat or heavy knife. Cut the seasoned butter into 4 long pieces and place one on each piece of chicken. Fold the flesh over the butter to enclose it completely, and secure with wooden cocktail sticks. The wing bone should protrude at one end of each cutlet. Season the flour with salt and pepper and roll each piece of chicken in it. Beat the egg lightly on a plate. Roll or dip the chicken in the egg, coating each cutlet completely; then roll each in the breadcrumbs. Heat the fat or oil to 160–165°C/320–329°F, and deep fry 2 cutlets at a time until they are golden-brown and cooked through. Drain thoroughly and keep hot while frying the remaining two. Place the cutlets on a warmed serving dish with the bones overlapping in the centre. Remove the cocktail sticks and garnish with lemon wedges and parsley before serving.

FRITOT OF CHICKEN

4–6 helpings

1 cold cooked chicken

fat *or* oil for deep frying

MARINADE

a slice of onion
a sprig of parsley
2 × 15ml spoons/2 tablespoons
    olive oil
1 × 15ml spoon/1 tablespoon
    lemon juice

1 × 2.5ml spoon/½ teaspoon dried
    mixed herbs
salt and pepper

BATTER

100g/4oz flour
125ml/¼ pint tepid water
a pinch of salt

1 × 15ml spoon/1 tablespoon
    vegetable oil
2 egg whites

GARNISH

parsley sprigs

Cut the chicken into joints. Remove the skin and any excess fat, and place the joints in a deep bowl.

Make the marinade. Chop the onion finely with the parsley, and mix together with the other marinade ingredients. Pour it over the chicken joints and allow to stand for 1½ hours, turning them occasionally.

Make the batter by mixing the flour, water, salt, and oil together until smooth. Beat well, and allow to stand for 1 hour. Then whisk the egg whites until stiff, and fold into the batter.

Drain the chicken joints, dry well with soft kitchen paper, and dip each piece in the batter. Fry the joints in hot fat or oil until golden on all sides. Drain on soft kitchen paper.

Garnish with parsley, and serve with Tartare sauce.

CHICKEN CHASSEUR

4–6 helpings

1 roasting chicken
salt and pepper
25g/1 oz flour
1 × 15ml spoon/1 tablespoon
  cooking oil
50g/2oz butter
3 tomatoes *or* 1 × 15ml spoon/1
  tablespoon concentrated tomato
  purée

25g/1oz onion *or* shallot
175g/6oz button mushrooms
150ml/6fl oz dry white wine
275ml/11fl oz chicken stock
1 sprig each of fresh tarragon,
  chervil, and parsley

Divide the chicken into 8 serving portions. Season the flour with salt and pepper, and use to dust the portions. Heat the oil and butter in a frying pan, and fry the chicken pieces until tender and browned all over, allowing 15–20 minutes for dark meat (drumsticks and thighs), 10–20 minutes for light meat (breast and wings). When tender, remove from the pan, drain on soft kitchen paper, and transfer to a warmed serving dish. Cover loosely with buttered paper and keep hot.

Skin and chop the tomatoes if used, and the onion or shallot. Put the onion or shallot into the pan, in the fat in which the chicken was cooked, and fry gently without colouring. Meanwhile, slice the mushrooms, add them to the pan, and continue frying until they are tender. Pour in the wine, and add the chopped tomatoes or the tomato purée and the stock. Stir until well blended, then simmer gently for 10 minutes. Chop the herbs and add most of them to the sauce. Season to taste.

Pour the sauce over the chicken, sprinkle with the remaining herbs, and serve very hot.

Chicken Chasseur

CHICKEN WITH WALNUTS

4 helpings

4 × 15ml spoons/4 tablespoons
cooking oil
200g/7oz shelled walnuts (whole *or*
pieces)
4 whole chicken breasts
15g/½oz cornflour

a pinch of salt
a pinch of sugar
2–3 × 15ml spoons/2–3
tablespoons soy sauce
200ml/8fl oz water
100g/4oz button mushrooms

GARNISH

fingers of toast

Heat the oil in a heavy-bottomed saucepan. Fry the walnuts gently in the oil for 2–3 minutes until golden-brown. Remove them, and drain on soft kitchen paper.

Skin and dice the chicken breasts. Fry the meat in the pan, turning gently until light golden on all sides. Mix the cornflour, salt, sugar, soy sauce and water to a smooth paste, and add the mixture to the pan. Slice the mushrooms and add them. Cook all these ingredients together very gently for about 10 minutes or until the meat is just tender. Stir the mixture during cooking, to prevent it sticking to the bottom of the pan. Remove from the heat, stir in the walnuts, and serve immediately. Garnish with fingers of toast.

THE WALNUT.

CHICKEN À LA KING

—— 4 helpings ——

350–500g/¾–1lb cooked chicken
   meat
1 red pepper
175g/6oz button mushrooms
250g/8oz long-grain rice
50g/2oz butter

4 × 15ml spoons/4 tablespoons
   whisky
salt and freshly ground black
   pepper
a pinch of garlic powder
200ml/8fl oz double cream
1 egg yolk

Dice the chicken meat and put to one side. De-seed the pepper and slice it thinly. Trim and slice the mushrooms. Boil the rice for 12–15 minutes until tender, drain thoroughly, and keep hot.

Melt 25g/1oz of the butter in a frying pan and, when foaming, add the pepper and fry quickly for 2–3 minutes. Stir in the mushrooms, and cook gently for another 2 minutes. Put to one side. In a second pan, melt the remaining butter, add the diced chicken meat, and fry gently, turning as required, until well heated through. Pour on the whisky, set alight, and shake the pan to distribute the flames. When they die down, season the chicken well with salt, pepper, and garlic powder, and simmer until nearly all of the juices have evaporated. Stir in most of the cream, and bring gently to boiling point, stirring all the time. Blend the egg yolk into the remaining cream, and add a little of the cooking liquid from the pepper and mushrooms. Add the pepper and the mushrooms to the chicken, then stir in the yolk and cream. Re-heat gently without boiling until the sauce thickens a little. Pile on to a warmed serving dish, and surround with a ring of the rice. Serve hot.

Overleaf
From the back, clockwise
Poultry Hot Pot (page 29), Chicken à la King (above) and
Chicken with Walnuts (page 16)

DEVILLED CHICKEN

1 helping

1 poussin *or* chicken joint
salt and pepper
a pinch of ground ginger
a pinch of mustard powder

1 × 5ml spoon/1 teaspoon chopped
parsley
1 × 5ml spoon/1 teaspoon chopped
shallot
1 × 10ml spoon/1 dessertspoon
cooking oil

Split the poussin, if used, along the back, open it out, and skewer it into a neat flattish shape. Season to taste with salt, pepper, ginger and mustard, and sprinkle the parsley and shallot over it. Allow to stand for about 1 hour, turning occasionally so that the meat absorbs the varous flavours. Brush with oil. Grill for 20–30 minutes or until tender, turning 2 or 3 times while cooking so that the outside is lightly browned. Serve very hot.

GINGER.

CHICKEN CASSEROLE

6 helpings

1 chicken *or* 6 small chicken joints
salt and pepper
25g/1oz flour
125g/5oz streaky bacon, without
  rinds

50g/2oz mushrooms
25g/1oz shallots
50g/2oz butter *or* fat
500ml/1 pint chicken stock

Joint the chicken. Season the flour, and dip the joints in it. Cut the bacon into strips 1.25cm/½ inch wide, slice the mushrooms, and skin and chop the shallots. Heat the fat in a flameproof casserole and fry the bacon, mushrooms, and shallots gently. Add the chicken joints and fry them until golden on all sides, turning them as required.

Add enough hot stock just to cover the chicken pieces. Simmer for 1–1½ hours or until tender. Re-season if required. Serve from the casserole.

BRAISED CHICKEN WITH PARSLEY

50g/2oz parsley sprigs
100g/4oz butter
salt and pepper

2 spring chickens
150ml/6fl oz water
275ml/11fl oz double cream

GARNISH

lemon wedges   parsley sprigs

Cut the stalks off the parsley sprigs and chop the leaves coarsely. Soften 50g/2oz of the butter, season, and mix with half of the parsley. Place half the mixture in the body of each bird. Melt the remaining butter in a large pan, put the chickens in the pan, and brown them lightly all over. Add the water, cover, and cook gently for 40 minutes or until tender. Remove the chickens and halve them. Put in a serving dish and keep hot. Add the cream to the stock in the pan and cook over low heat, stirring until the sauce is smooth. Add the remaining parsley, and re-season if required. Pour the sauce over the chicken and garnish with lemon wedges and extra parsley sprigs.

Note If spring chickens are not available, use 1 roasting chicken, stuff it with the butter and parsley mixture, and cut it into quarters after cooking. Allow 10–15 minutes extra cooking time.

Braised Chicken with Parsley

CHICKEN BRAISED WITH CHESTNUTS

—— *4–6 helpings* ——

400g/13oz chestnuts
1 small chicken
25g/1oz butter
1 × 15ml spoon/1 tablespoon olive oil *or* other good vegetable oil

125ml/¼ pint soy sauce
425 ml/17fl oz water
4 slices ginger root
2 spring onions
a pinch of salt

Remove the shells and skins of the chestnuts. Wipe the chicken and halve it. Cut each half into 4 pieces without removing any bones. Heat the butter and oil in a saucepan and fry the chicken until golden-brown. Add the soy sauce and water, and bring just to the boil. Remove the pan from the heat. Mince or grate the ginger and chop the onions. Add them to the saucepan with the skinned chestnuts and salt. Cover, and simmer for 1 hour or until the chicken is tender and the chestnuts have broken up and are thickening the sauce.

RAGOÛT OF CHICKEN

4–6 helpings

1 chicken
1 onion
125g/5oz ham *or* bacon
50g/2oz butter

50g/2oz flour
500ml/1 pint chicken stock
salt and pepper

Joint the chicken. Skin and slice the onion. Dice the ham or bacon. Melt the butter in a saucepan and fry the joints in it until lightly browned; them remove and keep hot. Fry the sliced onion lightly in the same fat, Sprinkle in the flour and brown it slowly. Add the stock, season carefully, and stir until boiling. Replace the joints in the sauce, add the diced ham or bacon, cover with a tight-fitting lid, and cook gently for 1 hour or until the chicken is tender. Re-season if required.

Serve the chicken with the sauce poured over it.

ONION.

CHICKEN CASSEROLE WITH LEMON

6 helpings

6 chicken joints *or* 3 chicken
   quarters
salt and pepper
50g/2oz butter
1 × 15ml spoon/1 tablespoon oil
1 medium-sized onion
1 lemon

4 × 15ml spoons/4 tablespoons
   plain flour
250ml/½ pint chicken stock
2–3 bay leaves
1 × 5ml spoon/1 teaspoon caster
   sugar

Halve the chicken quarters, if used. Season the joints well with salt and pepper. Heat the butter and oil in a frying pan, and fry the joints until golden-brown all over. Transfer to a casserole.

Skin and slice the onion and slice the lemon. Put the onion in the frying pan and cook gently for about 5 minutes until tender. Sprinkle in the flour and cook for 1 minute. Blend in the stock and bring to the boil, stirring all the time. Add the sliced lemon, bay leaves, sugar, and salt and pepper to taste. Pour into the casserole and cover. Cook in a fairly hot oven, 190°C/375°F/Gas 5, for about 1 hour until the chicken is tender. Remove the casserole lid 5 minutes before the end of the cooking time.

Chicken Casserole with Lemon

CHICKEN WITH RICE

1 chicken *or* 4 chicken quarters
chicken giblets *or* 2 chicken stock
   cubes
2 × 15ml spoons/2 tablespoons oil
40g/1½oz butter
250g/8oz button onions

100g/4oz button mushrooms
1 bay leaf
50ml/2fl oz dry white wine
200g/7oz canned red peppers
175g/6oz long-grained rice
salt and pepper

GARNISH

chopped parsley

If using a whole chicken, cut into quarters. Cook the giblets in 1 litre/2 pints of water for 40 minutes, or make stock with the cubes. Put the oil and 25g/1oz of the butter in a large pan, add the chicken, and brown gently all over. Remove to a plate. Prepare the onions and mushrooms. Place them in the pan with the oil, bay leaf, wine, and 150ml/6fl oz of the stock. Cover, and cook for 15 minutes. Remove, measure the stock, and make up to 500ml/1 pint with the remaining stock.

   Drain the peppers and cut them into strips. Heat the remaining 15g/½ oz butter in a frying pan and cook the rice in it gently for about 2 minutes. Add the onions, mushrooms, stock, wine and peppers. Season well. Place in a casserole, arrange the chicken on top, cover and cook in a moderate oven, 180°C/350°F/Gas 4, for 1 hour, by which time most of the stock will have been absorbed. Arrange the rice on a heated serving dish with the chicken on top and sprinkle with parsley.

POULTRY HOT POT

4–6 helpings

1 boiling fowl with giblets
3 rashers streaky bacon, without
    rinds
salt and pepper

nutmeg
2 onions
2 carrots
275ml/11fl oz chicken stock
3 × 10ml spoons/3 dessertspoons
    flour

GARNISH

2 × 15ml spoons/2 tablespoons
    chopped parsley

Joint the fowl and remove the skin. Place the joints, with the liver and heart, in a casserole or saucepan with a tight-fitting lid. Cut the bacon into strips, and add with the salt, pepper, and nutmeg. Prepare and dice the onions and carrots, and add with the stock. Cover, then either cook in a fairly hot oven, 190–200°C/375–400°F/Gas 5–6, or simmer for about 2–2½ hours until tender. Blend the flour with a little water, add some of the chicken stock, and return to the pan. Stir it in, and cook until thickened. Serve sprinkled with parsley.

Boiled rice makes a good accompaniment.

BOILED FOWL.

CHICKEN WITH CUCUMBER SAUCE

4–6 helpings

1 chicken
1 lemon
1 bay leaf
salt and pepper
1 small onion

1 cucumber
25g/1oz butter
25g/1oz plain flour
2 × 15ml spoons/2 tablespoons
single cream

GARNISH

1 × 15ml spoon/1 tablespoon
chopped parsley

Place the chicken in a large pan with just enough water to cover it. Pare the lemon rind thinly and add to the pan with the bay leaf, salt, and pepper to taste. Bring to the boil, cover, and simmer for 1½–2 hours until the chicken is tender. Skin and chop the onion. Dice the cucumber. Lift the chicken from the pan, cool slightly, and strip away the skin. Strain 250ml/½ pint stock from the pan for the sauce. Return the chicken to the pan and keep hot.

Melt the butter in another pan, add the onion and cucumber, and cook for 1 minute. Stir in the flour, gradually blend in the stock, and simmer gently for 10–15 minutes. Cool slightly. Squeeze a little juice from the lemon, and add to the sauce with the cream and salt and pepper to taste.

Lift the chicken on to a serving dish and coat with sauce. Sprinkle with parsley.

Chicken with Cucumber Sauce

HINDLE WAKES

6 helpings

1 × 1.5kg/3lb chicken
350ml/14fl oz chicken stock

grated rind and juice of ½ lemon
a blade of mace (optional)

STUFFING

175g/6oz prunes
50g/2oz onion
125g/5oz soft white breadcrumbs
1 × 5ml spoon/1 teaspoon dried
   mixed herbs

50g/2oz shredded suet
1 × 15ml spoon/1 tablespoon
   Demerara sugar
salt and pepper
1 × 15ml spoon/1 tablespoon malt
vinegar

GARNISH

6 soaked prunes (see Method)

lemon slices
parsley (optional)

Make the stuffing first. Put the prunes in a basin, cover with cold water, and leave to soak overnight. Reserving 6 for the garnish, stone and chop the rest. Skin the onion and chop it finely. Mix it with the prunes, breadcrumbs, mixed herbs, suet, sugar, salt, and pepper. Sprinkle the mixture with the vinegar and mix together. Use the stuffing to fill the body cavity of the chicken.

Truss the chicken and place it in a large saucepan or flameproof casserole. Bring the stock to the boil, add the lemon rind and juice, and a blade of mace. Pour the stock over the chicken. Bring to the boil, reduce the heat, cover, and simmer for 1½ hours until tender. Drain, and garnish with the reserved prunes and lemon slices. Arrange in lines along the back of the chicken, using cocktail sticks to secure the garnish. Parsley sprigs can also be used. Serve with the stuffing and hot lemon stock.

CHICKEN WITH CURRIED RICE

1 chicken with giblets	150g/5oz long-grain rice
1 carrot	2 large mild onions
2 sticks celery	100g/4oz butter
1 litre/2 pints (approx) chicken stock *or* water	1 × 15ml spoon/1 tablespoon curry paste
1 blade of mace	salt and pepper
6 black peppercorns	50g/2oz small onions *or* shallots

Place the chicken in a large saucepan with the giblets. Slice the carrot and celery, and add them to the pan with enough stock or water to cover the chicken. Add the mace and peppercorns, and cover with a lid. Simmer gently for 2 hours or until the bird is tender. Drain well. Reserve the stock.

Strip the flesh from the chicken, and slice it. Wash and drain the rice. Skin and slice the large onions. Heat 50g/2oz of the butter in a pan and fry the onions until lightly browned. Add the curry paste, mix well, and fry gently for 2–3 minutes. Add the rice and 750ml/1½ pints of the reserved stock. Season to taste, cover, and simmer for 15–30 minutes until the rice is tender and the stock is absorbed. When ready, remove the rice from the heat, and keep warm.

Heat the remaining butter in a frying pan and add the chicken pieces; fry gently until browned on all sides. Leave the butter in the pan. Add the chicken to the rice mixture and cook slowly until the rice is heated through again. Stir in a little more stock if necessary, and re-season if required. Place on a serving dish and keep hot. Skin and slice the small onions or shallots into rings. Fry quickly in the butter used for the chicken, and pile on top of the rice. Serve very hot.

CHAUDFROID OF CHICKEN

6 helpings

6 cooked chicken joints	lettuce leaves
125ml/¼ pint aspic jelly	3 sticks celery
375ml/¾ pint mayonnaise	2 hard-boiled eggs

GARNISH

stoned olives *or* gherkins	tomato wedges *or* slices

Remove the skin, excess fat, and bones from the chicken joints, keeping the pieces in neat shapes. Melt the aspic jelly, and leave to cool. Just before it reaches setting point, while still tepid, add three-quarters of the mayonnaise, and whisk in. Blend to a smooth consistency. Place the chicken joints on a wire cooling tray and coat with the mayonnaise sauce as soon as it reaches a good coating consistency. Arrange the lettuce leaves on a serving dish and place the chicken joints on top. Prepare and chop the celery, slice the eggs, and arrange these round the chicken. Spoon the remaining mayonnaise over the celery and egg. Garnish with the olives or gherkins and the tomatoes.

CURRIED CHICKEN SALAD

1 large cooked chicken
150ml/6fl oz mayonnaise
25g/1oz curry powder

500g/1lb (approx) natural yoghurt
salt and pepper
paprika

GARNISH

parsley sprigs   thin green pepper rings

Remove the cooked meat from the bones. Take off any skin or fat, and cut into small pieces. Mix the mayonnaise with the curry powder, stir in the yoghurt, and season to taste. Mix half the sauce with the turkey or chicken, arrange on a serving dish, and spoon the remaining sauce over. Sprinkle with a little paprika and garnish with the parsley and pepper rings.

PARSLEY.

CHICKEN MAYONNAISE

1 cooked chicken *or* 6 cooked
  chicken joints

275ml/11fl oz aspic jelly
425ml/17fl oz mayonnaise

GARNISH

pickled walnuts

pieces of red and green pepper

Joint the whole chicken, if used; remove the skin, excess fat, and
as much bone as possible, and trim the joints to a neat shape. Melt
the aspic jelly. When almost cool, blend 150ml/6fl oz of it carefully
into the mayonnaise. Beat well to blend thoroughly. Place the
pieces of chicken on a wire cooling rack, and when the sauce is a
good coating consistency, coat the pieces, using a large spoon. Cut
the pickled nuts and the pieces of red and green pepper into
attractive shapes for garnishing, dry well on soft kitchen paper,
and stick on the chicken with dabs of half-set mayonnaise. Melt
the remaining aspic jelly again if necessary; cool until it is on the
point of setting, and use to coat the chicken thinly.

TURKEY

ROAST TURKEY WITH CHESTNUTS

---

1 turkey
salt and pepper
1kg/2 lb chestnuts
275ml/11fl oz stock
50g/2oz butter

1 egg
single cream *or* milk
500g/1lb sausage-meat
2–3 slices fat bacon
fat for basting

Season the turkey inside with salt and pepper, but do not truss it.
Remove the shells and skins of the chestnuts. Stew them in the
stock for 1 hour, then drain and chop or sieve them. Melt the
butter and beat the egg, and add both to the chestnuts with
seasoning and enough cream or milk to moisten the mixture. Fill
the neck end of the bird with this chestnut stuffing, and the body
of the bird with seasoned sausage-meat or basic forcemeat. Truss,
and cover the bird with bacon. Roast for 15–20 minutes in a hot
oven, 220°C/425°F/Gas 7, then reduce to moderate, 180°C/350°F/
Gas 4, and cook for 20 minutes per 500g/1lb turkey weight plus 20
minutes, until tender. Baste well. Remove the bacon towards the
end of the cooking time to allow the breast to brown. Remove the
trussing string, and transfer the bird to a warmed serving dish.
  Serve gravy separately.

Roast Turkey with Chestnuts

TURKEY FRITTERS

4 helpings

400g/13oz sliced cold cooked
   turkey
50g/2oz ham *or* boiled bacon
1 egg

50g/2oz soft white breadcrumbs
2 × 5ml spoons/2 teaspoons
   chopped parsley
oil *or* fat for deep frying

Cut the turkey into neat pieces. Mince the ham or bacon very finely. Beat the egg until liquid. Mix together the minced ham, breadcrumbs, and parsley. Dip the turkey in the beaten egg and coat with the breadcrumb mixture. Press the coating on firmly. Heat the fat to 175–180°C/347–356°F, and fry the fritters until golden-brown. Drain and serve immediately.

DEVILLED TURKEY

4 helpings

2 cold cooked turkey legs
2 × 15ml spoons/2 tablespoons
   made English mustard

salt
a few grains Cayenne pepper
chilled pats of butter (optional)

Cut the legs in half at the joints. Score the flesh with lengthways slits cut down to the bone. Rub with the mustard, pressing it well into the slits. Season lightly with the salt and Cayenne pepper. Grill over moderate heat, turning as required, until crisp and brown. Top each joint with a pat of butter if liked, and serve very hot.

MUSTARD.

TURKEY WINGS IN GINGER SAUCE

4 helpings

8 turkey wings
salt and pepper

flour for dredging
oil for shallow frying

SAUCE

juice of ½ lemon
4 × 15ml spoons/4 tablespoons
  chopped stem ginger in syrup

2 × 15ml spoons/2 tablespoons
  medium-dry sherry
25g/1oz butter

Remove and discard the pinions from the wings. Skin the wings by holding them firmly in soft kitchen paper or a cloth, and peeling off the skin. Season the flour with salt and pepper. Roll the wings in the flour. Heat the oil in a frying pan to a depth of 1.25cm/½ inch. Fry them gently, turning as required, until tender and golden-brown on both sides. This will take about 17–20 minutes. Remove from the pan, drain on soft kitchen paper, and keep hot while making the sauce.

Put the lemon juice, stem ginger, sherry, and butter in a small saucepan, and bring to the boil. Place the turkey wings on a heated serving platter and pour the sauce over them.

Serve with buttered noodles or plain boiled rice.

Turkey Wings in Ginger Sauce

CASSEROLE OF TURKEY LEGS

—— *4 helpings* ——

2 turkey thighs *or* drumsticks
flour for dredging
50g/2oz butter *or* margarine
1 × 15ml spoon/1 tablespoon
  cooking oil
1 medium-sized onion

1 large clove of garlic
125g/5oz mushrooms
400g/13oz canned tomatoes
2 chicken stock cubes
2 × 5ml spoons/2 teaspoons dried
  marjoram
salt and pepper

Sprinkle the turkey legs with flour. Heat the fat in a large
flameproof casserole, add the oil, and when hot, put in the turkey
joints. Fry gently, turning as required, until browned on all sides.
Drain on soft kitchen paper, Skin and chop the onion, add to the
fat remaining in the casserole, and fry gently for about 5 minutes,
until softened. Skin, crush, and add the garlic. Quarter the
mushrooms, and add to the pan with the tomatoes and their liquid.
Add the crumbled stock cubes, marjoram, and seasoning to taste.
Return the turkey joints to the casserole, cover, and simmer, or
cook in a warm oven, 160°C/325°F/Gas 3, for 1½ hours or until the
meat is very tender.

Remove the meat from the bones, and serve from the casserole.

BLANQUETTE OF TURKEY

4 helpings

1 small onion
turkey bones, raw *or* cooked
1 blade of mace
salt and pepper
600ml/1 pint water (approx)
40g/1½ oz butter

40g/1½ oz flour
350–450g/¾–1lb cooked turkey
    meat
a pinch of nutmeg
2 × 15ml spoons/2 tablespoons
    cream *or* top of milk
1 egg yolk

Skin and slice the onion. Place the turkey bones, onion, mace, and seasoning in a pan. Add about 600ml/1 pint water, cover the pan, and simmer for at least 1 hour. Strain, and reserve 450ml/¾ pint of the stock.

Melt the butter in a pan, stir in the flour, and cook for 2 minutes without browning. Gradually stir in the reserved stock. Bring to the boil, stirring all the time, and cook for 10 minutes. Dice the turkey meat. Add the nutmeg and turkey pieces to the sauce, and re-season if required. Heat thoroughly for about 20 minutes. Mix the cream or milk with the egg yolk, and stir in a little of the hot sauce. Return the mixture to the pan, and heat gently without boiling for about 5 minutes.

Serve hot with boiled rice.

Overleaf
From the back, clockwise
Turkey Salad (page 52), *Turkey Mousse (page 49)* and
Devilled Turkey (page 41)

BRAISED TURKEY

1 turkey (5–6kg/10–12lb approx)
2 onions
2 carrots
1 leek
4 sticks celery
1 small turnip
2 rashers streaky bacon without
  rinds
100g/4oz butter *or* margarine

1.5 litres/3 pints chicken stock
125ml/¼ pint red wine
a pinch of dried thyme
1 bay leaf
6 parsley sprigs
salt and pepper
25g/1oz flour
2 × 15ml spoons/2 tablespoons
  double cream

GARNISH

chopped parsley

Choose a large pan which will hold the turkey, or halve the bird lengthways, and place each half in a large deep roasting tin. (In this case, divide the other ingredients equally between the tins.)

Prepare and chop all the vegetables and the bacon. Melt the butter or margarine in the pan, and fry the chopped vegetables and bacon, turning as required, until lightly browned all over. Add the turkey, pour the stock and wine over the bird, and add the herbs and seasoning. Cover tightly with a lid or foil, and simmer very gently for 3½–4 hours. (If cooking the halved bird in 2 tins, reduce the cooking time to 2–2½ hours.) Baste occasionally with the liquid in the pan while cooking.

When the bird is tender, remove it from the pan, and keep hot. Strain the remaining cooking liquid into a smaller pan. Discard the vegetables and herbs. Blend the flour to a smooth paste with a little cold water, and stir it into the stock in the pan. Place over gentle heat, and stir until the sauce thickens. Stir in the cream, and re-heat, but do not boil. Place the bird on a heated serving platter and sprinkle with chopped parsley. Serve the sauce separately.

TURKEY MOUSSE

250g/8oz cooked turkey breast
   meat
275ml/11fl oz double cream
275ml/11fl oz chicken stock *or*
   broth with fat removed

1 × 15ml spoon/1 tablespoon
   gelatine
3 egg yolks
salt and pepper
4 × 10ml spoons/4 dessertspoons
   mayonnaise

GARNISH

watercress sprigs

small lettuce leaves

Remove any skin, gristle, and fat from the turkey. Mince the meat finely. Whip the cream until semi-stiff, then chill. Put 100ml/4fl oz of the stock or broth in a heatproof container, and sprinkle on the gelatine. Leave until softened. Meanwhile, beat the egg yolks lightly and stir into the rest of the stock or broth. Season if required, and cook gently in the top of a double boiler until the custard thickens. Remove from the heat, and turn into a chilled bowl. Dissolve the softened gelatine by standing the container in a pan of hot water. Stir until dissolved; then stir it into the egg custard, blending well. Blend the minced turkey meat in thoroughly. Stand the bowl in a basin of cold water or crushed ice, or chill until the mousse mixture begins to thicken at the edges. Fold in the chilled whipped cream and the mayonnaise at once. Turn into a wetted 1 litre/2 pint mould and chill until set. Turn out on to a platter, and garnish with watercress sprigs and small lettuce leaves.

Sweet and Sour Turkey Salad

250g/8oz canned pineapple rings
a pinch of salt
a pinch of pepper
a pinch of dry English mustard
a pinch of caster sugar
4 × 15ml spoons/4 tablespoons
   corn oil
1 × 5ml spoon/1 teaspoon soy
   sauce

1 × 15ml spoon/1 tablespoon cider
   vinegar
500g/1lb canned bean sprouts
250g/8oz cold cooked turkey
1 small green pepper
100g/4oz carrots
50g/2oz whole blanched almonds

Drain the juice from the pineapple and reserve 1 × 15ml spoon/1 tablespoon for the dressing. Put the salt, pepper, dry mustard, and sugar in a mixing bowl and add the corn oil. Blend together. Gradually add the reserved pineapple juice, the soy sauce and vinegar, and beat well. Drain the bean sprouts and add them to the dressing. Cut the turkey meat into pieces and add it to the bowl. Remove the membranes and seeds from the pepper and cut the flesh into thin strips. Scrape the carrot, and cut into thin strips. Add both to the bowl. Toast the almonds lightly. Cut the pineapple into segments and stir into the salad with the almonds. Transfer to a salad bowl or dish. Chill before serving.

TURKEY SALAD

375g/12oz cold cooked turkey
1 hard-boiled egg
2 sticks celery
1 × 15ml spoon/1 tablespoon corn
  salad oil

1 × 15ml spoon/1 tablespoon
  vinegar
salt and pepper
6 × 15ml spoons/6 tablespoons
  mayonnaise
lettuce leaves

GARNISH

selection of gherkins, capers,
  anchovy fillets, radishes, and
  watercress

Cut the turkey into neat pieces. Separate the egg white and yolk.
Chop the celery and egg white. Mix all these together with the
corn oil, vinegar, and seasoning. Leave to stand for 1 hour. Stir in
the mayonnaise. Sieve the egg yolk. Pile the turkey, celery and
egg white on a bed of lettuce, sprinkle with the sieved yolk, and
garnish as liked. Chill before serving.

ROAST TURKEY.

DUCK & GOOSE

DUCKLING IN RED WINE

4 helpings

1 duckling
salt and pepper
2 medium-sized onions
1 bay leaf
250ml/½ pint red wine
100g/4oz bacon
1 × 10ml spoon/1 dessertspoon
   cooking oil

400ml/16fl oz stock
1 medium-sized carrot
2 sticks celery
grated rind of 1 orange *or* lemon
100g/4oz button mushrooms

Cut the duckling into quarters and season well. Skin and chop the onions finely, and put into a bowl with the duck quarters, bay leaf, and red wine. Cover, and leave to marinate for 2 hours. Remove the duck portions from the wine and dry on soft kitchen paper; strain and reserve the liquid.

Chop the bacon. Heat the oil in a pan and cook the bacon gently for 3–4 minutes. Add the duckling and brown it all over. Drain well, and put in a casserole. Heat the stock and pour it into the casserole. Cook in a moderate oven, 180°C/350°F/Gas 4, for 15 minutes.

Meanwhile, prepare and slice the carrot and celery. Add to the casserole with the grated rind, mushrooms, and the reserved marinade. Cover, and cook for 1½–2 hours until tender. Skim off any surplus fat before serving.

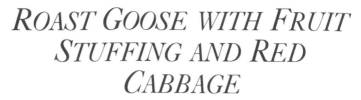

ROAST GOOSE WITH FRUIT STUFFING AND RED CABBAGE

6–8 helpings

375g/12oz prunes
1 goose with giblets
1.5 litres/3 pints water
½ lemon

salt and pepper
500g/1lb cooking apples
1 × 15ml spoon/1 tablespoon
   redcurrant jelly

RED CABBAGE

1.5kg/3lb red cabbage
50g/2oz butter
50g/2oz Demerara sugar

75ml/3fl oz water
75ml/3fl oz malt *or* cider vinegar
salt and pepper

Soak the prunes overnight. Remove the giblets from the goose and simmer them in 1.5 litres/3 pints water until the stock is reduced by half. Put to one side. Weigh the goose and calculate the cooking time at 20 minutes for every 500g/1lb. Remove the excess fat usually found around the vent. Rinse the inside of the bird, then rub the skin with lemon. Season with salt and pepper. Remove the stones from the prunes and chop the flesh. Peel and core the apples and chop them roughly. Mix with the prunes and season to taste. Stuff into the body of the bird. Place in a very hot oven, 230°C/450°F/Gas 8, reduce the temperature immediately to moderate, 180°C/350°F/Gas 4, and cook for the calculated time.

Meanwhile, prepare the red cabbage. Shred finely. Melt the butter in a large flameproof casserole. Add the sugar and cabbage and stir well. Add the water, vinegar, and seasoning, cover and cook in the bottom of the oven for about 2 hours, stirring occasionally.

When the goose is cooked, drain off the excess fat, retaining the juices in the pan. Make a slightly thickened gravy using the reserved stock and the juices. Add the redcurrant jelly and stir until it melts.

Serve the gravy and red cabbage separately.

Roast Goose with Fruit Stuffing and Red Cabbage

DUCK AND ORANGE CURRY

1 duck
salt
2 × 15ml spoons/2 tablespoons
  margarine *or* vegetable oil
2 large onions
2 cloves garlic
1 × 2.5ml spoon/½ teaspoon
  cardamom seeds
1 × 10ml spoon/1 dessertspoon
  finely chopped ginger root

1 × 5ml spoon/1 teaspoon cumin
1 × 5ml spoon/ teaspoon turmeric
1 × 10ml spoon/1 dessertspoon
  ground coriander
1 × 5cm/2 inch piece cinnamon
  bark
6 cloves
freshly ground black pepper
750ml/1½ pints unsweetened
  orange juice

Joint the duck into 4 or 6 pieces, removing any surplus fat. Season well with salt. Heat the margarine or oil, add the duck, and fry for 15–20 minutes, turning frequently. Remove the duck from the pan and put to one side. Skin and chop the onions and cloves of garlic, add them to the fat left in the pan, and fry until transparent. Add all the spices and the orange juice and bring to the boil, stirring all the time. Replace the duck in the pan, cover, and simmer for 1¼–1½ hours. Season with a little extra salt if required.

Serve with rice and other curry accompaniments.

DUCK WITH GREEN OLIVES

500ml/1 pint water
giblets of 1 duck
2 carrots
2 medium-sized onions
bouquet garni
salt and pepper

1 duck
2 × 15ml spoons/2 tablespoons
    goose, duck *or* chicken fat
2 slices stale white bread
24 stuffed green olives
3 small carrots

Put the water in a saucepan with the duck giblets but reserve the liver (this can be used for another dish). Cut up the carrots and onions roughly and add them to the pan with the bouquet garni and seasoning to taste. Simmer uncovered for about 40 minutes to obtain about 375ml/¾ pint well-flavoured stock. Put to one side.

Meanwhile, season the inside of the duck. Heat the fat in a heavy flameproof casserole, put in the duck, and brown it on all sides. Reduce the heat, cover the casserole, and cook slowly for 15 minutes. Remove the duck, joint it, and return the joints to the casserole. Grate or crumble the bread, sprinkle it over the duck, and strain the stock over the dish. Plunge the olives into boiling water for 1 minute, then add them to the casserole. Slice the small carrots thinly, and add them also. Cover the casserole, place over low heat, and simmer for 45 minutes.

Serve with boiled rice.

THE OLIVE.

SALMI OF DUCK

4 helpings

1 Spanish onion
1 duck *or* trimmings from 2 cold
  roast ducks
fat for basting
40g/1½oz butter

25g/1oz flour
350ml/14fl oz beef stock
12 stoned green olives
salt and pepper

If using a whole duck, skin and slice the onion into a roasting tin, put the prepared duck on top, baste with hot fat and roast in a fairly hot oven, 190–200°C/375–400°F/Gas 5–6, for 1–1½ hours or until tender.

Melt the butter in a small saucepan, add the flour, and cook slowly until the flour browns. Stir in the stock and simmer until thick. Keep warm. Remove the trussing string from the roast duck and cut it into small joints. Add either the freshly roasted or the cold duck to the sauce with the olives; season, and re-heat thoroughly. Sieve the onion or chop it finely, and add to the duck. Drain off the fat from the roasting tin and add the sediment to the sauce.

The salmi can be served on croûtes of fried bread with the sauce and olives poured over them.

Salmi of Duck

DUCK IN ORANGE AND CLARET

1 cold roast duck	500ml/1 pint beef stock
25g/1oz butter	1 orange
1 onion	100ml/4fl oz claret
25g/1oz flour	salt and pepper

Carve the duck ready for serving. Melt the butter in a saucepan, skin and chop the onion finely, and fry it in the butter. Stir in the flour and cook gently until brown. Add the stock, stir until boiling, and simmer for 10 minutes. Pare the rind of the orange, cut it into very thin strips, and squeeze out the juice from the orange. Add the rind to the sauce with the orange juice, claret, and pieces of duck. Season to taste. Simmer very gently for 30 minutes. Arrange the meat on a serving dish and pour the sauce over it.

ROAST DUCK.

DUCK OR GOOSE ON CROÛTES

---

4 helpings

375g/12oz trimmings of roast goose
   or duck
2 onions
50g/2oz butter
25g/1oz flour
500ml/1 pint beef stock
2 cloves

1 blade of mace
6 allspice berries
6 small mushrooms
salt and pepper
8 croûtes fried bread 8.75cm/3½
   inches in diameter

Cut the meat into neat pieces. Skin and chop the onions finely,
melt the butter in a saucepan, and fry the onions until lightly
browned. Stir in the flour and cook slowly until nut-brown. Stir in
the stock and boil for 10 minutes. Tie the spices in muslin and add
with the mushrooms to the pan. Season to taste, and simmer
gently for 20 minutes. Arrange the pieces of meat neatly on the
croûtes, remove the spices from the sauce, re-season if required,
and pour the sauce over the meat.

   Serve apple sauce separately.

DUCK WITH GREEN PEAS

4–5 helpings

1kg/2lb fresh peas
12 button *or* spring onions
250g/8oz rashers streaky bacon
50g/2oz butter
1 duck

425ml/17fl oz chicken stock
bouquet garni
salt and pepper
sugar
1 small round lettuce (optional)

Shell the peas and put to one side. Prepare the onions, and parboil them with the bacon. Drain. In an ovenproof casserole or saucepan large enough to hold the duck, melt the butter, add the onions and bacon, and toss quickly until light brown in colour. Remove from the pan. Put the duck in the pan and brown it well all over, then remove it.

Put a third of the stock into the pan and boil down to half its quantity, then add the remainder of the stock with the duck, onions, bacon, peas, and bouquet garni. Season lightly with salt and pepper and a pinch of sugar. Bring to the boil, then cover the pan and cook in a fairly hot oven, 190°C/375°F/Gas 5, for about 45 minutes. Baste from time to time.

Remove the duck and place on a serving dish; surround with the peas, onions, and bacon. Reduce the cooking liquor by boiling, then pour it over the duck.

A quartered lettuce may be added to the duck and peas when cooking; in this case, cut and serve the duck in quarters, and garnish with lettuce leaves as well as the other vegetables.